Love Letter to an Imaginary Girlfriend

Kenny Knight

Love Letter to an Imaginary Girlfriend

Shearsman Books

First published in the United Kingdom in 2022 by
Shearsman Books Ltd
PO Box 4239
Swindon
SN3 9FN

Shearsman Books Ltd Registered Office
30–31 St. James Place, Mangotsfield, Bristol BS16 9JB
(this address not for correspondence)

www.shearsman.com

ISBN 978-1-84861-814-5

ACKNOWLEDGEMENTS
Some of the poems in this collection have been previously published in
Clutter, International Times, Litter, Shearsman magazine, The Deadbeat Hotel,
The Journal, Long Poem Magazine and *The New European.*

Contents

*Love Letter to an
Imaginary Girlfriend*

for
Melisande Fitzsimons
Helen Foster
&
Sara Elizabeth Smiles

Molly

For too many nights to number
I have whispered my family name
through this thin wall
a name as common as Christmas
have spoken to my mother
have called myself Molly
in the wild seafaring tongue
have dreamed myself
out of the egg
grown feathers and taken
my first steps into the sky

and now here I am
dipping my beak
into the world's
largest rain puddle
shaking the ocean
off my back
leaving the ground
and the cracked dome
I once called home
to cross the green
and the blue
on wings as long
as my grandmother's.

Heidi

For Heidi Green

Heidi is leaving town
to live in a village
in the north of Aragón
is emptying one house
to fill another
is moving like winter into spring
like summer into autumn.
A voice drifting on the wind
in the middle of the night
a traveller hunched over a table
out on the Atlantic
watching cups slide
like disembodied ice skaters.

Heidi is leaving the island
on which this town is built
leaving the sea
but not the moon
making travel plans
like the gypsies of the sky
leaving in an old pair
of sleep-walking boots
as the sun rises
on the east side of town
Leaving here
to live in the mountains
to read Lorca
to make sketches
to paint Spain
the colour of Segovia's guitar.

Mongolia

For Matthew Carbery

When I glance at the big screen
in room three hundred and twenty
I can see you talking to people
sitting in four rooms in four universities
two in Wales
and two in other parts of England.
Your book lays on the table between us
set in the last century
tracking the long poem
in American Literature
with or without roots in Whitman.

In room three hundred and twenty
there's a map of the world
hanging on the wall behind your chair
the sea is a lighter blue
than the cover of your book
night is not here yet
there's a map I can't see
wrapped around the world and shifting.

If I could travel around the world
I would travel across it
in a weather balloon
if only travelling were as simple as that
the thought of departure and arrival.
If only it were as easy
as getting out of a chair
and walking across the room to Mongolia
to see the snow leopards
or deconstructing molecules
a short step
or less than half a dozen footsteps

quicker than nipping
over to the supermarket
shopping for tea bags and soya milk.

In room three hundred and twenty
I look across the blue
of the pond to America
and think about writing
a poem that long
three thousand miles of soggy paper
a poem that begins in Honicknowle
and ends on Olson's doorstep in Massachusetts.
When I write I take things from everywhere
like a magpie and twist them
and when you slip psychedelics into the mix
in the form of magic mushrooms
I wonder how many
past and current trippers
there are seated around these five tables.
Two that I know of for sure
sitting next to each other
like Albert Hoffman and Aldous Huxley.

Making Mary Shelley

I made you out of bits and pieces
out of this and that
the heart of a frog
the legs of a waitress
stuck paper all over your body
tattooed with old words
gave you language
made you multicoloured
added a second coat
a hat and gloves.
Your fingernails were the colour
of a wedding dress
your mind a jigsaw of land and sea
your gaze filled to the brim with innocence
your body made out of science-fiction
out of superglue and Superman comics
the shoes of the road
the face of Mary Shelley
you were as tall as marijuana
on a night out in the rain.

On Christmas Eve
I wrapped you in gift paper
left you under the tree
sleeping on pine needles
and in the morning
fed you sunflower seeds
filled you with mud from everywhere
rain from a dozen thunderstorms
lashings of spit sprinkled with sawdust.

I taught you to play the piano
to appreciate jazz and Americana
gave you a star sign

one slipper in Capricorn
one in Sagittarius
gave you a bicycle pump
the fingers of a short story writer
the eyes of the crowd
cloned you for the supermarket
made you out of the rags of capitalism
made you as durable as vanilla.

Reading Paul Celan

For Christina Peters

The surrealistic diner
at the other end of the terrace
pours Christmas pudding
over her Christmas lunch.
Birds fly under the roof of the cafe
a foghorn practices the shipping forecast
a child leaps out of the bushes of memory
seashells pinned to his ears.
For entertainment we listen
to the theme tune from Harry Potter
look out to sea
as the sun shines a yellow eye
over the distant shoreline
of Friday afternoon.

We have expensive taste in poetry
we dunk teabags into teapots
reading to each other and the hecklers
of the sky in German and English.
Lottie lays at your feet
a black and white rug under the table
doesn't interrupt the conversation
doesn't bark or tut
in German or English
when a fight breaks out
at the other end of the terrace
in the middle of reading Paul Celan.

The sky let's go of its grief
a soft rain falls
on Lottie's black and white coat
falls on handbags and teddy bears
as the passengers

of a pram parked nearby
skip the formalities of bell ringing
launch into each other with gusto
knocking seven bells of featherweights
out of Harry Carpenter's punch bag
kicking salt and pepper pots
kicking sugar cubes across the floor
juggling spoons in the air
that fall through the air
words that shoot out of bodies
ricochet off tables and chairs
a little bit of off-screen drama
a brief interlude on Friday afternoon
somewhere between Tinside Pool
and a tin of Winalot in Christina's kitchen.

The day ages by the minute
by midnight it'll be
the mother of tomorrow
the clocks will go into labour
the prams will have moved off
with their wheels and bruises
the gift of peace
and quiet will return
and we'll turn the page
read some more Paul Celan
take brown and blue photographs
of autumn leaves falling
from the lighthouses of the sky
onto the dark landscape
and desecrated heart of the city.

After a couple of rounds
the sugar cubists depart
leaving us alone with Paul Celan
and the surrealistic diner
finishing her Christmas starter

and dessert in a photo finish
that no-one takes.

In another time and place
under the family tree
of a distant autumn
in a heart held together
by sugar cubes and loss
I imagine myself
out on the streets of a city,
a city much like this
which is a gateway
to somewhere else
a city which Louis Aragon
and Maurice Chevalier passed through
some years after Houdini
escaped the river's grip
a city which gave the world
A Curious Shipwreck
the Speedwell and the Beagle
seadog of evolution and Devil's Point
overlooking the sea, overlooking yesterday.

Sixty feet above the shoreline
to the east of Darwin's great landmark
we practice the art of multitasking
translating surrealism into English
drinking tea and coffee
under the shadow of Smeaton's Tower
under the pedals of a big wheel
from some giant bicycle we'll never ride.
Skirting the cold corpse of Christmas lunch
Lottie passes through the lunchtime crowd
like a ghost through butter
the sea moves towards us as if we were
the adopted children of King Canute
engaged in a futile rebellion of deckchairs

outclassed by the moon and the tide
cast as castaways in a parallel
Paul Celan movie someone else is making
making sandcastles out of nothing
out of narrative, out of language.

It was ducks not blackbirds

It was ducks not daffodils
or five pound notes that did it for me
thunderstorms in the teaching room
and a mad dash home
along Coombe Park Lane.
The streets were dry and I remember
crossing three roads without looking
but there weren't so many cars back then
there were some but not as many
as there were cats
in that book by T.S. Eliot
which I read some years later.
Cats lived out between the fields,
you could see their eyes at night
on the road to Modbury
or sitting on windowsills,
looking wise, looking intellectual
like Egyptian professors.
Cats working undercover,
infiltrating our lives
living rooms and sofas.

Out of breath
when I reached our house
I flung open the back door
looking for my mother
who stood alone washing dishes
at the kitchen sink.
She smiled and waved a greeting
her hand a glove of soap bubbles
and in my eagerness to share
I slipped and skated over words
as if they were made of ice
my mind and my mouth

filled with images of rain and feathers.
I had discovered something old and beautiful.
It was ducks not Dickinson that did it for me.

Forgetting to wipe my feet
I stepped into the house
stepped onto the doormat
as if it were a stage
a little bit of Lear might have crossed.
Without any preamble
I grabbed a broomstick
making my debut
on the Plymouth Poetry scene
to an audience consisting
of my mother and the family cat
and in the applause that didn't follow
I climbed the stairs to the quiet
of my room where I looked
out the window across the Tamar Valley
and in my imagination
sent an innocence of crows
flying north across the sky
to Woodland Wood
freewheeling across
the years yet to come
before turning west
into the last of the day's blueness.

It was ducks not Dylan
raindrops not rivers that did it for me.
It was a ripple of poetry on a pond
a blink of blue eyes
gazing down into still water.
It was nonsense verse
and nursery rhymes
not Hilda or Ogden Nash
it was a seed which grew underground

into a tall and slender bush of marijuana
it was the year I hit seventeen
the year I got serious about making
language out of language
and sometime after that
I recall my mother saying
there was more money
to be made robbing trains
then there was writing poetry
for Faber and Faber
and she was right
but I never wanted
to rob the midnight train to Adlestrop
never wanted to sell
free verse on the free market.
It was ducks not dollars that did it for me.

Letter to a Longhaired Girl

I had a pen friend
when I was at school
she was German,
it wasn't Christina,
it was Brunhilde
we met on the pages
of a teenage magazine
started writing to each other
in Nineteen Sixty Six
the year England won the World Cup
nine hundred years after losing it at Hastings.

I don't remember the name
of the city where Brunhilde lived
it could have been Düsseldorf,
Cologne or Munich.
A daughter of the Cold War
she could have lived
on a street close to the Wall
looking out of a Berlin window
looking out over the city
sometimes in the morning
sometimes in the evening
watching crows flying east
watching ravens flying west.

She could have been born in Baden Baden
so good they named it after New York.
There might have been
a photograph of herself
she sent in one of those letters
a black and white snapshot
taken outside a museum
in Brunswick or Ravenstein

a photograph smaller than a postcard
like one you'd use for flying out of a country.

I don't remember much
of what we wrote
we were young teenagers
so I must have mentioned
my newspaper round
must have told her
how I travelled to America
to play electric guitar
with The Honicknowle Blues Band
at the Fillmore West in San Francisco.

I don't know if she was tall
if she was blonde or brunette
all I know or remember
is that she spoke two languages
her handwriting was blue
she was left handed
to match her politics
she liked German Literature
and the American rock band, Steppenwolf.

The last time I wrote to Brunhilde
I told her I was smoking marijuana.
It must have been Nineteen Sixty-Nine.
It must have been rock and roll.
She wrote back
her words filled with concern.
I thought she'd be alright with that
somehow in my innocence.

We were fourteen or fifteen
when we started writing to each other
seventeen or eighteen when we stopped.

I think of her sometimes
while travelling through Europe
or drinking coffee
with Christina on Frankfort Gate.
She was my one and only pen friend
a stranger out of childhood
a native of Hanover
or the Black Forest
sticking stamps on envelopes
in the land of Wagner.

If she wrote to me now
would she talk
about her grandchildren
her home in Mönchengladbach
her holidays on the Rhine.
Would I tell her about
my life in the blue
my life out on the road
reading poetry all over the city.
My life waiting tables
looking for red and blue numbers
in a supermarket cafe
my nine to five existence
or last weekend on the moon.
And if we met by chance
say in a coffee shop in Heidelberg
would she remember
the name of that teenage magazine
or those letters she wrote
to a longhaired boy.
Would she look into the past
see herself scribbling
talking softly in two languages
talking to crows flying north
to ravens flying south
talking doorstep to doorstep

talking marijuana and Kurt Schwitters
talking pen to pen across Europe
to a longhaired girl living quietly
since Nineteen Sixty-Nine
on a suburban street
somewhere in Bavaria.

Crossing the Park to Connecticut

When the park
on the other side of the fence
comes out of winter's long sleep
we'll cross it like those travellers
searching for some sort of promise
in a movie set in the American west.
When we get there, wherever that is
there'll be no shoot-outs or bicycles
taking off into the sunset.
When we get there
across the park that is
we'll head up the slope
and hit the shops
exchange our pocket money
for superheroes and bags of sweets.
After stuffing ourselves
with gobstoppers and pineapple chunks
and filling imaginations with Flash Gordon
and Captain America
we'll go trekking in our plimsolls
and not quite teenage feet
slipping our slim bodies
and slimmer shadows
into the trees behind the old fort
where we'll play robbing the rich
while slowly heading west
to where the sun crosses the river
over in that land where Merlin
might have played the ukulele
in the Connecticut court of rock and roll.

Maybe when we get a little taller
we'll grow up to become newspaper boys
reading stories about rich men making war

maybe we'll go into town on Saturday nights
where we'll hang around
on one street corner or another
maybe we'll fall in love
with a gang of flower power girls
grow our hair long
move to New England or California.
Say goodbye to Mayflower Street.

Broken Windows

All people are your people
the people of the world
the people of the desert
the people of the rain
the people of the snow
the people of the fog.

All people have brown eyes
blue eyes and other colours
eyes that see the bright emptiness
of the moon through broken windows.

I can't speak
for the strangers from the stars
or the children who live there
nights and miles away from this land
where my family shelters
in a house by the sea.

The Queenfisher

for Sara Elizabeth Smiles

Out of mud comes beauty
out of the river
comes the queenfisher
flying home with a stickleback
making a bed on a cushion of bone.
She's got a hairstyle made for
a punk rock night in Bretonside.
She likes the Bus Station Loonies
X-Ray Spex and the Clash
she likes the Mississippi Mafia
Country Joe and the Fish.

When she hunts
she hunts amongst the ripples
puts make-up on her feathers
whispers to her brood
in the language
the rain speaks to the river.
I saw her last year
in an art gallery in Paris
last week looking out
of a window in New York.
When she comes to the Art College
I feed her lunch from the river
which runs to the west
of King's Tamerton.

When I delve
into some book of magic
laying on a table
in a library at the end of a river
I see a romantic out fishing

leaning over the riverbank to drink
making herself invisible to everything
but the wind and other queenfishers.

I close my eyes
take a breath of autumn
and she's gone
diving like a paintbrush.

Shadows on a Zebra Crossing

You remember
when the world
and everything in it
was a big toy that had wheels
which moved like magic
when you waved
and pointed and laughed
at the grown-up children
in the grown-up cars
when that giraffe
driving a steam roller
stopped to let the shadow
of a crow and a swan
fly over the zebra crossing
outside the greengrocer's
at West Park
back when you had
fire engines in your eyes
when you had
long conversations
with trains and buses.

You remember
back before love and peace
and the Vietnam war
when you walked
with a bunch
of teenage friends
along that path in the dark
looking down at the years
written in stone
looking down
at all kinds of flowers
growing on the doorsteps

of shopkeepers and nurses
growing in that garden
behind the walls of the church.

This was before
you became a newspaper boy
before you read the headlines
and the small print
before you became a beatnik
walking barefoot
in bohemian slippers
or a teddy boy
sniffing Brylcreem
back before you became
a mod
living next door
to a rocker
you remember
seeing cars
driving down the road
towards Marsh Mills
from the back garden
of a house on Derwent Avenue
cars made so small by the distance
you thought they were
like the cars
you played with at home
under the tree at Christmas.
You remember
seeing toy vans and toy trucks
toy motorcycles and sidecars
toy children on toy bicycles
toy mothers pushing toy prams
and in that moment of long ago magic
your eyes became the eyes of a wizard
a wizard playing the part of Gulliver
some sixty short

summer times gone passing
like those blue cars
chasing getaway cars
along the riverbank at Laira.

This must have been
the summer you saw
an old aeroplane
from World War Two
flying in the clouds at Crownhill
above the prefabs
on Shenstone Gardens
the summer you heard farmers
driving cattle to market
gates opening and closing
tractors on the radio
in your grandmother's cottage
at Langbrooke
about a dozen miles or so
from the zebra crossing
at West Park
where in Nineteen Fifty-Five
or Fifty-Six
the shadow of a crow
flew under the neck of a giraffe.

The Traveller

We were playing time-travellers
in a room on that street
between the prefabs and the park
your mother's house or maybe mine
half a lifetime ago, maybe more.

When a voice called your name
out in the darkness
you stopped playing dinosaurs
stopped playing cowboys
picked up your harmonica
and walked through the open window
never lifted a hand
or a parting word in the air
never paused to read the name
of the rock and roll group
I'd scratched into the condensation
on the glass
which drifted after you into the night
like a vaporous dog.

I waited and waited for your return.
It didn't come.
Is it like this for all of us
this feeling of loss.
Is it the same for the traveller
as it is for the one who closes the window.

All the Rooms of the World

It rained on the day we left Europe
rained all over England
on Frankfort Gate
on Melisande's flip-flops
on Normandy Way
on international conversations
on Portland Square
on the black and white chessboards
of kings and queens
playing stay or leave on Armada Way
on the headstones of Ford Park
the rooftop of the Continental Hotel
the cobbled streets of Bretonside
rained all over Brussels, all over Calais
and all through the night it fell
through trees bending in a breath of wind
passing through the sleep of travellers.

I huddled under an umbrella
in all of those places
and the rain spoke to seabirds
in the seaside town of Dover
spoke in the common language of the sky
falling on the white cliffs of Vera's song
spoke of distant landscapes
recalling thunderstorms in the hush of night
those first steps taken in childhood
in all the rooms of the world
signposts measured in miles and years
the long road to a land of refuge and bluebirds
all those moments of loneliness and regret
broken by a hand waving
somewhere under the sea
from the window of a train.

Falling in the Beautiful Dark

for Helen Foster

All my family want
is to live in the air
in a big house of feathers
live in a tree for two
with a couple of eggs
under a cloudy roof that leaks rain
with a green curtain that doesn't fall off
when summer slips over the skyline.

All my family want
is a home in the city
but if that home
were ever taken out
to make way for nothing
chopped down by a lumberjack
with a black belt in karate
or if it fell
into the arms of the beautiful wind
would we have somewhere else to go
a second home in the sky
somewhere to crash overnight
in a park or on a street
somewhere to make
space above the grass
and the undergrowth for us
and the next generation of eggheads
somewhere to shit on the traffic
somewhere where mammals
don't throw things out of the sky

but if we had to move
we wouldn't want to move
in spring or summer

move our shiny pickings
across the air
to a detached row of town houses
not until our young
had grown tall enough to roost
only then would we move
flying north to live
in wild domestic bliss
in some leafy suburb
a family treehouse in feather-land
overlooking a prime piece
of indigenous architecture
where we'd sing the city to sleep
sing to the sun falling from the sky
before dozing off in the moonlight
all snug and tucked-up
under a canopy of leaves
rocking in the beautiful dark
while the wind blows off the Atlantic
like one of Bob Dylan's songs.

Bird Song in a Variety of Colours

I don't know the name of the birds
who dropped out of the sky
to make a home for the spring
and the summer in the suburbs
of this bare-leafed city.
I can't see through
the sunglasses they wear
so have no idea whether they have
green or brown eyes to match
and guide them to the ground.

When they call to each other
they call in the key of blue
but sometimes purple
they like rock and roll
like me and my mates
left wings strumming
right wings like air guitars
they have feathers
the colour of traffic lights
a culture as old
as summer and winter
when they come to town
in March and April
they smuggle stories
of opium dens
fairy tales of dragons
bring the rustle of silk
the sound of wind chimes
muffled voices
behind bamboo curtains
a flock of Chinese
bird songs in the air.

The Wind Has So Many Names

Sometime last week somewhere in the city
in the world of finance and big business
a supermarket chain acquired Argos
for so many millions.
Somewhere in the world sometime after work
I went shopping with my old grungy purse
and for the first time my new black rucksack
which I filled with hazelnuts, a dead chicken
and a carton of soya milk,
unsweetened
unlike the silver spoon of recent news.
Sometime yesterday
somewhere here and there across the city
I walked unknowingly like so many others
under the headlines of the news
under the bare armed
and green sleeved branches of trees
under the arms and body of a cherry blossom
which fell from the earth like a proposal
or a premature Valentine.

Yesterday
somewhere in the city
I read letters in the *Plymouth Herald*
on the ongoing saga
of free speech and free verse
and in one of those letters
a Horsham Lane historian
quoted some of the greats
from the back catalogue
of English Literature
Alfred Lord Tennyson.
Robert Service.
Rudyard Kipling

o.k. so far.
Mark Twain.
Walt Whitman.
Surely not.
Surely American
like Longfellow and Dickinson
or like a parody paraphrasing Meatloaf
three out of five ain't bad.
Sometime after that
I declared myself Switzerland
and danced across the city
with the ghosts
of English Literature
and two Americans
danced with strangers in my hometown
and my hometown danced with Imogen
cheek to cheek in Woodland Wood
hand in hand with the cold fingers
of winter in Freedom Park.

The Road

Last year I began to mourn
for all the people I couldn't see
and more than that on sunny days
on the streets of the city
it was difficult to tell
if the crowd was moving
towards me or moving away.

And when sleep came
I passed into a land
of stereoscopic vision
and in one of those dreams
walking with an old friend
on the North Atlantic coast
out beyond Noss Mayo
where a finger
that could have been a voice
spoke or wrote in sand
to the shipbuilders of the night
to the lovers made of driftwood

and in that place
where shipwrecks are as common
as coffee on Saturday night
we toasted the moon and the ocean
with one of Europe's finest vineyards.
It was the last piece
of the scattered jigsaw
something sentimental
as the wind and the sea isn't
something broken and nomadic
reassembled on the road.

The Face That Launched
a Thousand Letters

Mad as a mud-pie
on Miss Havisham's table
I pop pills and potions
to keep the demons
under lock and zoo.
I hang around here
like a sentence.
I am short of coin
but rich in feathers.
I ride this surfboard
over the concrete
the rain comes and goes
falls on the newspaper heads
of gutter press pedestrians.
I see my eyes reflected
in the eyes of passing strangers
the windows of red-faced buses
my eyes fixed in a day long
day rider stare.
When the time comes
my retribution will be like poison
gushing out of a Trojan pen.
In my hand
I'll grip your letters like grudges
lurch like a lunchtime hit lady
hired by the bard.
Bianca calling from Stratford-on-Avon.

If I were Shakespeare
I'd convert your letters
into syllables the size of confetti.
if I were a policewoman
I'd superglue you to the ground

or handcuff you to my wrist
leave you hanging
like a shirt in the rain,
If I were the sun
or a waitress
I'd serve you ice-cream
turn you into a snowman.
If I had a white dress
to match my name
I'd slip in and out
of your nightmares
like the bride of Gollum.
If I were a petrol pump
I'd give a tank of four star
to any getaway driver
who'd read me some Paul Brickhill
play some Alice-in-Chains.
When the time comes
to tread the wind
to slip the ground off my feet
to slip these cobwebs
over my gown and shoulders
my retribution will be prolific.

On Reaching a Hundred

1

I don't remember
the Hundred Years War
and neither does the goldfish
but I do remember the night
we met on that Viking cruise.
It was love at a hundred yards.
It was leaf year
the year we vanished undercover
in a bed of magic
the year we made coffee
as much as possible
and not forgetting
those long lunches
we had in Tintagel
around that oddly shaped table
and that waitress at Guinevere's
who'd never heard of Maurice Chevalier.

2

This old bruise of romance
is my heart
blackened by your departure.
Send me a microphone
and a very long lead.
I've got so much to say.
I need someone to talk too.
How about meeting next week
under some constellation
that's ruled by a fish or a goat.

Venus will be in conjunction
with something or other
which'll make for good conversation.
Let's talk about make-believe.
Let's dropout from the egg and spoon race.
Go somewhere imaginary or stay at home
playing The Psychedelic Sheep of the Family.
Is your favourite progressive rock band
Paradox Lost or Marshmellow Milton.
Do you play the field or the triangle.
Have you ever lived in Hundred House.
Would you like to fall in love
with my telephone number.

3

I may not be a millionaire
by this time tomorrow
but I'd like to say
to the money spider
crawling across this poem
that my family tree
has roots in many languages.
Two of those trees
are the silver birch
and the monkey puzzle.
The silver birch
is snug and inviting.
The monkey puzzle
is a chatterbox and a flirt
and I'd like to say
standing out here on the breakfast aisle
that I never wanted to be
a part-time supermarket worker
selling corn flakes to the masses
all I ever wanted to do

was make narratives out of fragments
make sure I've got my reading glasses on
when I put a cross in that box.
I'd like to say after all these years
I've still got a crush on the waitress
feeding egg boxes into the cardboard bailer.
And I'd like to say
on reaching a hundred
that I used to have a thing for older women
and I'd like to add
that promises will be made
and promises will be broken
and I'd like to propose
on one knee or another
if we make it back from sleep
now November's here
after burning that telegram
and blowing out those candles
I'm in favour of the future
in favour of splashing out
on a small house
in the wilds of suburbia
a small house in a neighbourhood
of overgrown lawns
and I'd like to say
free speech and free verse is everywhere
but it won't buy you a ladder
to lean against a tree
won't buy you a lawn mower
or a short cut out of loneliness.
take it from last night's lipstick
the 13th Floor Elevators
aren't likely to be getting
anything psychedelic
from Santa Claus this Christmas.
Take it from the Four Marys
blueberries taste nice

so does instant coffee
and clotted cream
especially at the tip
of a silver spoon
and I'd like to say
in regards and sometimes regret
to yesterday wherever it may be
that the heart is a lonely place
prone to tears and sorrow
which needs to be filled
with sunflowers and poppies
and generations of children
the family home of the monkey puzzle
the family at the heart of the silver birch
the allotments of the sun
and the rain and the wind
the seeds and the roots of magic
the need to grow more trees
the need to fill more dance halls
and nightclubs with peace and quiet
and hundreds of weekend romances
dancing ghost-like in the nicotine dark.

Nightfall

I waited weeks for the voice
to resume this conversation
to talk to this recluse
waited for that train
for the lip reader of my dreams to call
I made speeches to strangers
hiding in the fog
sent flattery, flocks of words
Valentine cards on the Fourteenth of April.
Disguising myself as Hemingway
Gibran, Enzensberger,
a pin-up in reading glasses
or someone from Faber and Faber
praying for a stanza or two
or the T.S. Eliot Prize
to slip from your tongue.
Wooing you with a whisper
with the sound of language
the sound of magic
the crackle of white noise
the foghorn voices
of jazz singers on pirate radio
Taking a vow in the art
of loneliness and longing
on a marriage that comes and goes
sometimes in nothing but blue,
sometimes in darkness.
Taking down the minutes
before nightfall takes the day west.

In the fading light it wasn't snow
that fell from your hand on Tavistock Place
when we met somewhere between loss
and late afternoon on the last day of winter.

You were sitting in the waiting room
lost in thoughts of Christina
lost in the thrill of love
making or not making sense.
I couldn't stop a sigh becoming a ripple
as I touched the fingertips of your shadow
and your eyes opened and closed
like two blue doors
and your lips moved
like the wind passing through town.

A Short History of Woodland Wood

For Carl Eve

The last time I saw the moon
it was loitering in the sky
above the old library
and dungeons of Woodland Fort.
I was looking out of the window
of my new house
built by bricks pilfered
from the Great Wall of China.
My new house
skirting the edge of Woodland Wood.
The moon shining
on the shadows of tautology.

The last time I heard the throttle
of the crime reporter's motorbike
Hong Kong Gardens
was playing on the radio
on the new housing estate
on the corner of Woodland Wood Road.
Genghis Khan was hitching his pony
to a piece of post-modern sculpture,
an ambassador of dread
crossing the road to the butcher's shop.

The last time I sent you flowers
snow covered the ground like a shroud.
The sun was brighter than a blind man's eye
but the city was as dark as a tower of ravens.
The last time I saw the moon
it was passing over Woodland Wood
on Christmas Eve like a parody of summer.

Blue Gone Grey

Yesterday's certainty
has vanished in a trick of fog.
I now live in a world
devoid of body language
shuffle through crowds
some made of vapour
some made of skin.
Sometimes while crossing the road
I cannot see the green man.

Remembering my boyhood years
when I had the vision of a telescope
and could see across space
from Christmas Day to Capricorn
when I could see Blind Lemon Jefferson
playing at the other end of the street
somewhere in Freestone County
but not now
now I've got four blue eyes
four blue eyes gone to cloud
hesitant and unsure
I move through fog not made of vapour
blowing notes on a blues harmonica
to light my way

and on nights when there is fog
and visibility is next to nothing
I sit here in the quiet of my room
on the doorstep of the wild Atlantic
and read the love letters of Miss Havisham
to a sea monster playing jazz.

Reading in the Dark

Welcome back
it's good to see you again
it's been a long six weeks
without you here
I've missed your beauty
missed your smile
I could have lived quietly
in this fog for years
never knowing if you were
a fingertip away in the darkness
never knowing if you were
a friend or a stranger
until you spoke
never knowing
if we were in New York
or in that hospital
down by the railway line.

Welcome back
it's lovely to see your face
lovely to see the rain
lovely to sit here
reading in the dark
with the braille
taken from my eyes.

Olive

I have inherited my father's silence
I am having difficulty having conversations
with softly spoken people.
I have fallen asleep
to the sound of revellers
out in the weekend dark
only to awaken sometime after midnight
with the volume turned down
here in this house of wax.

It's odd this sudden sense of loss
I feel for the day-to-day soundtrack
of background noise.
I no longer hear you talking
to strangers in your sleep
or the riffs of the rock and roll
Hall of Fame candidate
playing Patterson Hood
and Mike Cooley songs
in the room above.
It's as if someone's
taken the language of things
out of the air
and reduced them to a whisper

For the last few days
I've felt like an extra
in a Charlie Chaplin remake.
All that's missing
from my life is sound
and the taste of dessert.

On the way into town tonight
I went shopping for olive oil

to squirt into my ears
went shopping for slapstick
bought half a dozen custard pies
to throw at the television screen
even though I cannot hear
the bullshit and the spin
that comes out of its deserted mouth
or the motorbike revving up
in the back lane
like a cover version of Steppenwolf.

The old age pensioners
passing by my house
on the way home
from darts or bingo
are mixing with headbangers
from my generation
in a Twenty First Century silent movie.
I am sitting here above the traffic
reading subtitles
in the darkness of my room
and gazing at the bright red lipstick
you're wearing tonight.
In the meantime while waiting
for Olive to work her magic
I tuck into a plate of spinach
and flick through my father's
old record collection
looking for something loud
and funky by John Cage.

Montevideo

For Melisande Fitzsimons

Before the words hit the microphone
at the poetry reading
the woman sitting next to me
falls asleep and starts talking to herself
in a language that sounds North European
but I don't know
I'm only guessing
I could ask Melisande
but it'll only make her tut
she's listening to Peter Gizzi
she says I fidget at poetry readings
but I'm only dancing to the distance
in the human voice.

I have two pens with me tonight
one writes poems for Melisande
the other writes poems for everything else.
With one pen I write about my father.
My father has gone but not to Montevideo.
My father never knew
how to pronounce Montevideo.
Meningitis at the age of seven
and deafness accounted for that.
With the other pen I write about
Maurice Chevalier and Sasha Distel.
I can't remember which one sang with Melisande.
I can't remember which one played the guitar.

Reading at the Beat Hotel

You can flog day trips
to any old universe
and rip-off some time-traveller
but not everyone
would be gullible enough to meet
Abraham Lincoln in North Hykeham
over a pint and a ploughman's lunch.

Seven days in France
on the face of it
for not much more
than the price of a pot of tea
sounded like a good idea
but not in the middle
of the Hundred Years War.

A fortnight on the set
of Doctor Who
hanging out with Daleks
and zipping off
in that telephone box
to see Pink Floyd
at the Roundhouse
on Chalk Farm Road
seemed like a better bet.

Meeting Andre Breton
was on the list as was reading
with Allen Ginsberg at the Beat Hotel.
Taking drawing lessons with Bosch or Escher
smoking three skinners in the Summer of Love
or getting Merlin to show you
how to wave a magic wand
and conduct the London Symphony Orchestra
sounded like a good night out in the past.

The second-hand Science-Fiction bookseller
had been thinking about time-travel
for the best part of twenty minutes
but the trouble with time-travel
is where do you go and what do you pack
and what's the weather going to be like
when you get to Atlantis
will it be sunny or foggy
or will there be rain
will sunglasses and cardigans
make you look inconspicuous
or anachronistic
after you leave the poppies
and the postcards
and the long dark nights behind
when the clocks go back in October.

Bloomsbury

If everyone I ever played
were to meet for lunch
we'd make quite a crowd
we'd need a table as big
and as long as a train
all the waiters and waitresses
would be my former co-stars
some coming back to haunt me
some to serve
some to play a part.

I have been so many people
I have made a living
playing the dead and the fictional
I have been an architect
and an archetype
I have considered leaving here
and vanishing into a crowd scene
somewhere in Bloomsbury.
In the last forty years
I have aged a dozen centuries
I have seen the ghosts
of myself and others
caught glimpses of fame
I have been a mugshot
on the cover
of a television magazine
a pin-up in your living room
a poncho made of dollars
the king of the flea pit
in a shaving advert
starring Santa Claus
the name up in lights
is there to remind me

who I was before I became
a drifter on the fringes of art.

For twelve years
I played a supermarket worker
in a retail soap opera
every night after work
I went shopping
with the wardrobe mistress.
Right now I'm making a living
playing an undercover cop
in an underground movie
I don't switch off when I get
back to me room
it's like I've been reincarnated
like one of those monks
on Sutherland Road
I've grown my hair long
to blend in with the smokers.
I no longer think about
making love to you
in that film which broke my heart
or that spaghetti western
that took more at the Box Office
than a riverboat gambler
bluffing the deck
somewhere out of shot
in someone else's movie.

Ace

For William Telford

It was Saturday night
the club was packed
like Dodge City in December.
At the table Carter and Kennedy
were keeping straight faces.
Derringers were tucked away.
There were dollars to be made
in the business of chance.
Through the corporate mist
I could see sixes and nines
taken and discarded by gamblers
with one eye on Tombstone
see empires and the faces
of presidents changing hands.

Over the rim of my glass
I could see you
scribbling in a notebook
with a pen that looked like the twin
of the pen
Cornelius Ramble may have used
when signing autographs
down at the Tumbleweed Hotel.

You were writing
a piece of flash fiction
a love letter to your sweetheart
a shopping list
a spaghetti western for a waitress
a short story of mods and rockers
rocking bat's-wing hinges
off nocturnal doors
down on the dusty

ghost town streets
of Wild Wish Hollow.

Underneath your breath
you were humming something
out of the jukebox of love and peace
that made me want to buy some flowers
and hit the road for San Francisco
head out through the bat's-wing doors
for the swinging sixties.

As I took a shot of sarsaparilla
a shot rang out
interrupting your writing
your undercover version of Scott McKenzie
and numerous other Saturday night conversations
around the bar.
As the six-gun smoke mingled
with dozens of cigarettes and reefers
I had flashbacks of cinema cowboys
shooting each other in Texas and Arizona.
of gunshots bouncing off
your bullet proof notebook.

On the edge of the poker table
I could see an Ace of Spades turning red
as an avalanche of cards hit the dust
like Wild Bill did over in Deadwood.
Through the window the sun was setting
like a diamond cashing out in the dark.
Calm as a weatherman in the middle of a storm
you slipped the notebook into a coat pocket
hung sunglasses over a suntanned face.
Looking out at the street
looking like a film star
in a vegan spaghetti western
or a silver haired stranger

in a cowboy novel
you nodded goodnight
while passing my table
and you were gone
like an ace in a hand of sevens
leaving the dead and the living
to bluff it out on both sides of the door.

I took a last sip of whisky
took my fingerprints and left
following your shadow down the street
to where you'd parked the truck.
After that we shuffled out of town
Emmylou keeping us company
for three or four minutes
with a little bit of country rock.

Lost in the narrative of departure.
Stargazing through the urban movie
on the windshield
the soundtrack of four star
underneath the hood.
Changing lanes
changing tracks
jamming along on the dashboard
and the steering wheel
to a harmonica out of Memphis
as we rode through the night
through green and amber
only stopping to make notes over coffee
on the outskirts of Abilene
where writers and truckers come and go
like conversations and blueberry muffins.

Dicing with Room Numbers

For Matthew Carbery

I like the red and yellow painting
with a dab of purple and a splash
of green on the left-hand side.
Dicing with room numbers
I come to the talk
on Twombly by mistake
but decide to stay and listen.

I have a small table
which is grey in colour
on which I place
these reading glasses
falling off this hand,
these blue eyes.

When I get home tonight
I'll switch on the record player
listen to some Chuck Prophet
some Bill Callahan
some Townes Van Zandt.
When I get home tonight
I'll rearrange the furniture
move the sofa
and the ironing board
take up ten pin bowling
take up juggling
when I get home tonight
I'll drop everything except art.

After eavesdropping on Twombly
I drop in on Buddy Holly
and Ornette Coleman
I mark academics smoking cigarettes

out on Cobourg Street with scores
as high as nineteen and twenty
as they camouflage themselves
with other smokers
in conversations of fog.

When I get home tonight
I'll switch on the radio
I'll read a biography
of Buddy Holly's.
I prefer Buddy Holly's
reading glasses to mine.

On the day the language died
there was an aeroplane crash
the day I started crowdfunding
to buy Van Gogh's portrait
of Don McLean on Amazon.
On the day my reading glasses
fell out of the sky
the moth made it possible
to see through the curtain
through two small windows of light.
Its wings are not red like the sea
it dances to Buddy Holly in pretty circles.

On the day I emerged
from my mother's body
ten years after the blitz
I could see the distance
of Christmas Day on my sister's face.
The November moon sent parts of the sun
shining down on seven and a half pounds
in old money
shining down on a body
made out of other bodies
made out of goosebumps.

October had just slipped out of the door
the first gurgle of poetry had just sauntered in.

On my family tree there aren't
any dinner ladies or ballerinas
but there are two blood sisters
they were both miscarriages of creation
I never met them or heard their voices
until I passed the point of beginning.
They were talking to each other
one night in my mother's house
interrupting the silence
after years of being quiet
they gave me breadcrumbs
they brought me jackdaws
sometimes at Christmas
they gave me a key to the house of jazz
they made me homesick for the sound
of Julie Andrews and Jimmy Garrison
they made me carry on writing
until the words are all
I want them to be on paper
write until there's nothing
to be gained by leaving
nothing to be lost by staying
nothing but a dozen people
and a tenor saxophone
laying down on its side
like John Coltrane sleeping.

When I go home tonight
I'll play some Robert Fisher
some Gregg Allman
some Tom Petty.
I prefer Tom Petty's
guitar playing to mine.

When I leave home tomorrow
I'll wear the reindeer jumper
Melisande gave me in April.
It makes me feel conspicuous.

When I get into a bit
of name dropping
I tell everyone
I'm an old friend
of John Cooper Clarke's
ex brother-in-law.
I've been famous
a couple of times
but not for as many minutes
as a tin of baked beans
in Andy Warhol's kitchen.

When I'm not shuffling cards
or the pages of a Dodge City western
I like dicing with room numbers
I like all kinds of things
I like my hometown
I like The Roundhouse
I like Global Village Trucking Company
but Boris and Brussels Sprouts
are two good reasons
for staying in Europe.

I spin the roulette wheel
with my lucky left hand
which takes me to a talk
on the Plymouth Poetry Mafia
the roulette wheel is still spinning
tell me if it stops on Geoffrey Hill
or Eric Dolphy.

The Mousetrap

At night the ghosts come out
and go shopping on the high street
you can almost hear an echo
of the clink of change
which takes me back
to shopping in Woolworths
and British Home Stores
back to paying two and six
for Jimi Hendrix in Pete Russells
back to hearing
young long-haired buskers
playing a medley of Donovan
and Woody Guthrie songs.
Folk singers making enough money
to see colours in the rain.

The last time a Victorian penny
fell into my pocket
must have been roundabout
Nineteen Sixty-Nine
loose change from the empire
before Bretonside became
a part of Europe
drinking cups of instant coffee
in the years before
the old Bus Station Cafe
became a night out
in the Hollywood Hills
a bar code towering above the Viaduct
no longer a pilgrimage for day trippers
no longer an articulated hotel.
The long-distance lorry drivers long gone.
I walk here still
approaching sixty-eight

but not too many
of these strangers know me
a tall silver-haired
psychedelic pensioner
shuffling through town.

Now the crowds are thin
and getting thinner
how long will it be before
this wildlife park for scavengers
becomes a museum
of scantily dressed mannequins
before the fat cat race
is a home movie
on a computer screen
a rock and roll catalogue
a department store
on the dining room table
a shopping mouse
eating out of my hand
above a fish and chip shop
on the edge of the sea.

Love Letter to an Imaginary Girlfriend

My girlfriend was born
in Fleet Western Lodge
quite close to Modbury
in Nineteen Fifty-Two.
She made her childhood home in Laira
playing on the riverbank
underneath the plum trees
watching trains and cars
racing the river back to town and the sea
leaving only mud and an old wooden ship.
The ribs of a Viking.

My girlfriend and I met one afternoon
under an umbrella in the rain
quite close to Camels Head
or closer to Camels Head
than anywhere else.
The night we got married
my girlfriend drove straight from church
into the honeymoon that is the Blue Monkey.
When we made it back home to Ernesettle Green
she taught me the esoterics of how to make art
how to make pancakes
how to unravel narrative and loss
how to woo sleep out of darkness.

My girlfriend played viola and saxophone
showed me how to dance to rock and roll
and other stuff
she knew the names of guitarists
from all over the world
and where to score weed
and where hitch-hikers went for Christmas.

After many years of happiness
autumn came and with it
my girlfriend gave me a choice of leaves
and I chose the hand of the willow
and we made love
and made paintbrush faces
under the constellation of Matisse
and when night fell she played
a little bit of Sugarcane
a little bit of Monk
a little bit of wind
breath and oboe
and she took me waltzing
across a dance floor of leaves
sometimes barefoot
sometimes in size six shoes
sweeping me off my odd socks
blue and green floating above the traffic.

Last Night

For Annie Jenkin

Here on the outskirts
somewhere beneath the stars
on a balcony in the trees
an owl hoots above the car horns
calling out to welcome the moon
and the mouse that moves in the shadows.

Your hand touches my fingertips.
The fog lifts a wispy eyebrow
drifts like plankton across field and lawn.
A rocket that can only dream of space
sparkles over the streetlights
falls unseen like a diluted nightmare.

On the last minute of the year
you flick the head of some dead king
up into the darkness, close your eyes
counting sheep or cardigans.

Here on the outskirts
the house mumbles to itself
small avalanches of soot and dust
and other rumblings
stretch from room to room.

The wind, indigenous to everywhere
brings a touch of the international
rocking pirate radio waves across the Atlantic
bringing the breath or other lands to these shores.
The windows chatter away in French.
It is winter now they say.
The sun has grown as distant as last night's lover.

Here on the outskirts of town
somewhere beneath the trees
we slip into Sixteen
and wait for the voice
of the owl to call again
a sound as old as midnight
lovely and haunting
bringing a premonition of sleep
and other delights.

Supermarket

When you reach
the end of the roadworks
leave your sandwich board
and sermons at the gate
when you reach amber
leave your packed lunch for the seagulls
your collected graffiti
your haikus cut off in mid syllable
your notebooks and suburban narratives
to the handclappers in the crowd
yesterday's words old as autumn
a montage of couplets and one liners
in plumages of chalk
all lit up under a September moon.

When you reach the end of your shift
traffic may be heavy
in the car park at sunset
and tomorrow when you select
a nightmare of modifications
in the supermarket or an item
from the short list of virtue
please wait in line
and play long electric guitar solos
to the crowd, to entertain us
practice it leaning against the archaeology
like you were waiting for Beckett
ten years to pass or fish and chips.

Silver and Red

You open the door
come in out of the sun
close it and move deeper
into the house of scissors
the sky seen through the window
looks as white as your skirt
as blue as your eyes
which are hidden under a fringe
of brown hair which hangs
and drops over your shoulders.

I sit here facing the mirror
watching you run your fingers
through another man's hair
watching your lips move
sometimes without sound
or none that reaches me.
I think yet again
of the vanity of men
while waiting for you
to call my name
in that time I read a story
in the *Daily Mail*
which I quickly drop
back onto the table
as if my fingers
and my senses had been burned.

And then I see your lips move
and then my long hair
falls to the ground
summer has gone
and now it's autumn
I know as the days

reach into October
that leaves will fall
all over the city
all over the land
but much sooner than that
someone else
some long-haired stranger
will sit where I sat
will take my place in the mirror.

And if I never see you again
what I'll remember most of all
will be your red fingernails
your smile in the mirror
and me stripped of language
smiling shyly back.

Here and There

I bought a bottle of red wine
and a box of Cobra
at the supermarket on Wednesday afternoon
smack in the middle of the consumer storm
in the madness that is Christmas
I took my grungy purse out of the pocket
of black charity shop trousers
the purse held together by safety pins
luck and circumstance, like this life
which is a jigsaw of scattered moments.

Lost and in love with the idea
of some mythical tomorrow
I slip out of this moment
and find myself fifty miles away
on the steps of the Dinosaur Café.
In the Dinosaur's window
my reflection becomes forty years younger
my short grey hair hangs long and brown
and in that instant the woman at the checkout
picks up the Cobra and looks me in the eye
like a barmaid in a spaghetti western
and asks if I've had enough birthdays to booze.
I fidget myself back to reality
show her my bus pass
before slipping back again
into a Pink Floyd moment –
searching for old loves
I drift through a back catalogue
of honeymoons, brown eyes, white dresses,
see one particular smile
so Saturday afternoon
the smile of a girlfriend
I married in another life

she meets me under the clocktower
picking me up in a dress
as colourful as Friday night traffic
a fan in one hand
a bunch of wildflowers in the other
slashing the air and my senses
catching my heart in a butterfly net.
Gazing from brown into blue
I tumble into that avalanche
shifting here and there, now and then
I recall the colour of your lipstick
and in the instant
I pick up the bottle of red wine
in a toast to the past
the woman at the checkout
lays three or four coins across my lifeline,
reading my palm
a postcard of morse
on the tip of a finger.

Bianca

One of your hands
looks like a high heel.
Kick it off your fingers
kick the world
around the park.
Dance like you're one
of the grand-daughters
of the Tiller Girls.

The first time I saw you
you reminded me of Isadora.
Have you come to save the world
from being taken over by politicians
are you the long-lost sister
of Clark Kent
or a graduate
fresh out of drama school
playing an undercover cop
blending with the crowd.

Did you leave a passport
between the pages of a novel
so you could slip
back home at nightfall
with only your shadow
dancing quietly by your side.

Bending your body like that
you look like you're about
to leave town on a surfboard
the tallest tall dark stranger
in the world
bowing your head
to the wind and the rain

the travellers and the fairy tales
to the five-star sun
shining in your dark eyes
to the feathers
dropping off to sleep
on your Saturday night shoulders.

Sparrow

Take me back
to the wind
to that tree
spreading its shade
beneath the blue
watercolours of the sky

let me out
of this room
out of this cage
of lost feathers
out of this paint box
of congested art

take me back
back to my cluttered house
in the labyrinth of numbers.

Glossary

Many locations in Plymouth and its environs are mentioned in the poems, and we thought they needed referencing for those who do not know the area. Likewise, cultural references that seem unexceptional to the author and the publisher probably do need some explanation for younger readers, the existence of Wikipedia notwithstanding.

LOCATIONS IN PLYMOUTH

Blue Monkey — pub in the St Budeaux district of the city. It burned down in 2006.

Bretonside — location of Plymouth bus station.

Crownhill — district immediately to the east of Honicknowle (q.v.)

Ernesettle Green — open space in Ernesettle, west Plymouth, near the River Tamar.

Ford Park — cemetery in west Plymouth, near the Argyle football stadium.

Freedom Park — located next to the old Freedom Fields hospital, where the author was born.

Honicknowle — district where the author grew up.

King's Tamerton — suburb of Plymouth.

Laira — S.E. Plymouth, with rail yards.

Pete Russells — indie record store, much beloved by those of an alternative persuasion in the 1960s and '70s.

Smeaton's Tower — a former lighthouse relocated to Plymouth Hoe, overlooking the Sound. Something of a symbol of the city.

Tinside Pool — open-air lido, off Plymouth Hoe; featured on the cover of the author's previous book *A Long Weekend on the Sofa*.

West Park — in Honicknowle.

Woodland Wood — near Honicknowle.

Woodland Fort — in Honicknowle; featured on the cover of the author's first book, *The Honicknowle Book of the Dead*.

PLYMOUTH STREETS

Armada Way — main thoroughfare on the edge of the city centre.

Broomball Lane — A country lane which runs from Honicknowle to the hamlet of Weston Mill.

Cobourg Street — northern edge of the City Centre, by the University.

Coombe Park Lane — in Honicknowle.

Frankfort Gate — on the western edge of the City Centre.

Horsham Lane — in Honicknowle.

Mayflower Street — on the eastern edge of the City Centre.

Shenstone Gardens — a former cul-de-sac of pre-fabs in the 1960s, between Honicknowle and Crownhill

Sherford Crescent — in Honicknowle.

Sutherland Road — between the railway station and Mutley Plain, where, oddly, the publisher lived between the ages of 5 and 11.

Tavistock Place — on the eastern edge of the City Centre, opposite the University.

LOCATIONS NEAR PLYMOUTH

Calstock — Cornish village on the Tamar shore.

Devil's Point — promontory overlooking the Sound.

Dinosaur Café — This café is in Exeter, some 40 miles east of Plymouth, and serves good Turkish food. The publisher used to live 10 minutes' walk away.

Langbrooke — a row of cottages found at the end of a country track, close to Ermington – where the author's Grandmother used to live.

Modbury — small coastal town to the east of Plymouth.

Noss Mayo — coastal village to the east of Plymouth.

Tamar Valley — the River Tamar marks the western boundary of Plymouth, and serves to mark the border between Devon and Cornwall in its lower reaches.

PEOPLE AND OTHER PLACES

Adlestrop — a village in the Cotswolds, but also the title of a famous poem by Edward Thomas, published in 1917.

Alice in Chains — American grunge-rock band, active from 1987.

Gregg Allman — American rock singer and songwriter (1947–2017) and member of the Allman Brothers Band.

Louis Aragon — French surrealist poet, Communist, and member of the resistance (1897–1982). He was in Plymouth in 1940, having been evacuated after the fall of France.

Beagle — the ship in which Darwin travelled around the world.

Paul Brickhill — Australian fighter pilot and author of a number of books on World War 2, including *The Great Escape, The Dam Busters,* and *Reach for the Sky.*

Bill Callahan — American singer-songwriter , a.k.a. Smog (b. 1966).

Canute, King — a.k.a. Cnut; Danish King of England 1016–1035; also King of Denmark from 1025 and Norway from 1028. Famously sat on his throne on the seashore and commanded the waves to retreat (although the story dates from the 12th century, and was intended to show him demonstrating that he knew the limits of his regal powers).

Paul Celan — German Jewish poet (1920–1970) born in Romania, who lived in Paris for most of his adult life and produced some of the greatest poetry in German in the 20th century.

Maurice Chevalier — French singer and entertainer (1888–1972), best known outside France for his appearance in the movie, *Gigi.*

Ornette Coleman — important American composer and jazz musician (1930–2015).

Mike Cooley — American singer-songwriter (b. 1966); founding member of the Drive-By Truckers.

Country Joe and the Fish — American band from the late 1960s, best remembered for their anti-war song, 'I-Feel-Like-I'm-Fixin'-to-Die Rag'.

Curious Shipwreck, A — book by Plymouth poet, Steve Spence (Shearsman Books, 2010).

Sacha Distel — French crooner, and jazz guitarist (1933–2004).

Eric Dolphy — influential American jazz musician (1928–1964),

Emmylou — i.e. Emmylou Harris, American country and western singer-songwriter (b. 1947).

Robert Fisher — singer-songwriter, and founding member of Willard Grant Conspiracy (1957–2017).

Peter Gizzi — US poet, b. 1959.

Global Village Trucking Company — alternative British band from the 1970s, founded by James Lascelles (b. 1953) and intermittently active since. One studio album, one live.

Buddy Holly — seminal American rock'n'roll artist (1936–1959).

Patterson Hood — American singer-songwriter (b. 1964); founder of the Drive-By Truckers.

Isadora — Isadora Duncan (1878–1927), an American dancer who had a starry career in Europe, and was briefly married to the Russian poet, Sergei Esenin. She died in Nice, when her long flowing scarf was caught in the wheel of the car in which she was being driven, and broke her neck.

Don McLean — American singer-songwriter (b. 1945), responsible for (among others) 'American Pie' and 'Vincent'.

Scott McKenzie — American singer (1939–2012), most famous for the single, 'San Francisco' (1967).

Melisande — Melisande Fitzsimmons, Plymouth poet.

North Hykeham — town in Lincolnshire.

Olson — Charles Olson, influential American poet (1910–1970), and godfather of the Black Mountain poets.

Tom Petty — American rock singer and songwriter (1950–2017), and leader of Tom Petty and the Heartbreakers.

Chuck Prophet — American singer-songwriter (b. 1963).

Kurt Schwitters — German Dada artist and writer who lived in exile in England 1887–1948. His work with collage (the results of which he called *Merz*) was groundbreaking.

Speedwell — a ship that accompanied the Mayflower to America in 1620; however it turned back before getting there and returned to Plymouth.

Steppenwolf — American-Canadian rock band, mostly remembered today for their singles, 'Born to be Wild' and 'Magic Carpet Ride' (both 1968).

Tiller Girls — British female dance troupe, with origins dating back to the late 19th century, who were famous in the 1950s and early 1960s.

Twombly — Cy Twombly, American artist (1928–2011).

Townes Van Zandt — American singer-songwriter (1944–1997).

X-Ray Spex — British punk band from the late 1970s.

Lightning Source UK Ltd.
Milton Keynes UK
UKHW041619060722
405447UK00001B/11